CAVES

A TRUE BOOK

by

Larry Dane Brimner

Children's Press®

A Division of Grolier Publishing

New York London Hong Kong Sydney
Danbury, Connecticut

An ice cave

Subject Consultant
Peter Goodwin
*Science Teacher, Kent School,
Kent, Connecticut*

Reading Consultant
Linda Cornwell
*Coordinator of School Quality
and Professional Improvement
Indiana State Teachers
Association*

Author's Dedication:
*For my friends at Scott Libby
Elementary School,
Litchfield Park, AZ.*

*The photograph on the cover
shows a limestone cave. The
photograph on the title page
shows a sea cave.*

Library of Congress Cataloging-in-Publication Data

Brimner, Larry Dane
    Caves / by Larry Dane Brimner.
        p.   cm. — (A True book)
    Includes bibliographical references (p.).
    Summary: Describes the different kinds of caves, how they are formed,
and the wildlife that lives within them.
        ISBN 0-516-21567-1 (lib. bdg.)   0-516-27189-X (pbk.)
        1. Caves—Juvenile literature.   [1. Caves.] I. Title. II. Series.
GB601.2.B75   2000
551.44'7—dc21   99-058037
                                                                          CIP
                                                                           AC

GROLIER
PUBLISHING

Contents

Explorers in a
limestone cave

Beneath the Surface

Deep down, beneath the world of sunshine, is the dark world of caves. Caves are hollows, or openings, in the surface of the Earth. Some are so small that one person cannot enter them easily. Others are enormous, with rooms bigger than football fields!

Caves are found in many parts of the world.

Huge caves form slowly over millions of years. But new caves are being formed all the time. They are found in almost every part of the world, and they are constantly changing.

There are several kinds of caves: sea caves, river caves, ice caves, lava tubes, sandstone caves, and limestone caves.

Sea caves form along the shores of oceans and large

A sea cave

lakes. They are made by powerful waves pounding against the cliffs that line the shores. These huge waves break away loose pieces of rock and, over time, a cave begins to form.

The action of rivers or streams can create caves, too. At a bend in the river, the current of water can wear away a huge hole in a cliff face. As time passes, the riverbed drops, leaving a cave high in the side of the cliff.

In some parts of the world,
glaciers—rivers of ice—flow
slowly downhill. When the sun
melts some of the ice on the
surface of a glacier, ice caves
start. The meltwater seeps

An ice cave

deep into cracks in the glacier
and then flows as a stream
underneath. On its way, the
stream of meltwater carves
out tunnels and rooms.

Lava tubes are made when
a volcano erupts. First, lava—

A lava tube

melted rock—spills down the sides of the volcano. On the surface, the lava cools and hardens, but underneath, the melted rock still gushes.

Eventually, the liquid lava stops flowing from its source. As the lava flows away, it leaves behind a tube-shaped cave.

In southwestern Colorado, people known as the Anasazi— a Navajo word meaning "ancient ones"—built dwellings of stone in huge sandstone caves. Sandstone caves are usually not deep. They are made when rainwater or a stream flows down the side of a sandstone cliff. The

The Anasazi people built dwellings in the huge sandstone caves of Mesa Verde, Colorado.

water breaks down the material that holds the sandstone together. Then it washes the grains of sand away to leave a shallow cave.

Limestone caves may be huge and may contain spectacular rock formations.

When most of us think of caves, however, we are thinking of limestone caves. These are the caves with the enormous rooms. Strange rock formations hang from their ceilings and tall pillars rise up from their floors. Some of these caves have tunnels that lead to other caves, looping and winding for miles and miles.

Limestone caves form only under certain conditions. Let's take a closer look at these interesting caves.

How Limestone Caves Form

Limestone is made when tiny ocean organisms, or living things, die and their skeletons settle on the ocean floor. Their skeletons are made of a mineral called calcite. Over millions of years, a thick layer of this mineral builds up. Sand, mud, and dead plant life may settle

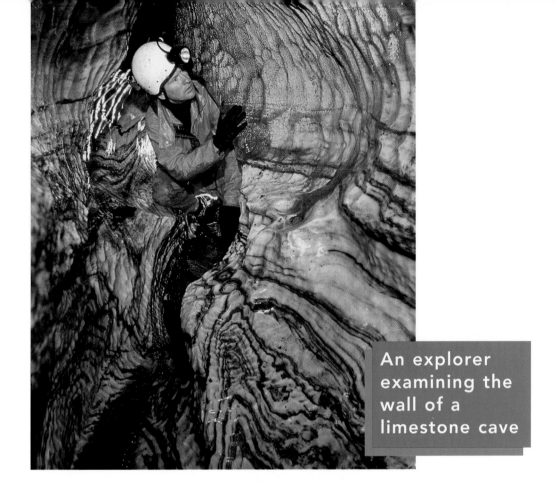

An explorer examining the wall of a limestone cave

on top of it, and other minerals may seep into it. At the same time, the great weight of the ocean water presses down on the calcite particles and

Tiny shells form a carpet of calcite as they collect on the ocean floor. Over millions of years, they become cemented together into limestone (left). These are limestone formations under the sea (below).

cements them together, forming a rock called limestone.

The limestone may remain under the ocean floor for millions of years. Then the sea level may drop, or forces within the Earth may thrust the sea floor above the surface of the waters. When this happens, the limestone is ready to begin the slow process of becoming a cave.

Limestone caves are also called solution caves. Rain is needed to make them form. As rain falls to the Earth, it picks up carbon dioxide. Carbon dioxide is the gas that animals and humans breathe out. Carbon dioxide is also given off by dead or decaying plants.

The rain picks up more carbon dioxide as it seeps into the soil and through the layers of dead plants. The rain and carbon dioxide mix together to become a weak acid called carbonic acid. This acid water slowly dissolves the calcite in limestone.

Geologists—scientists who study the Earth's soil and

rocks—believe that limestone caves begin to form where the acid water reaches the water table. The water table is the top of an underground layer of water-soaked soil. Below the water table is groundwater, which supplies springs and wells with water.

The acid water mixes with the groundwater, soaking the limestone below the water table with carbonic acid. It slowly eats away the limestone, but does not affect rocks made

A limestone cave may have slow-moving water flowing through it for centuries until the last of the ground-water drains away.

of stronger minerals. Carbonic acid dissolves only limestone. Eventually, the groundwater drains away and air enters the hollow left behind. A limestone cave has been made.

Inside Limestone Caves

Once air enters a limestone cave, the cave stops growing bigger. This happens because much of the carbon dioxide in any remaining water escapes to the air so the water no longer has enough acid in it to dissolve the limestone.

Once air enters a limestone cave, the remaining groundwater deposits calcite back into the cave, creating amazing rock formations.

Nature's work, however, is not over yet. As the water becomes less acidic, it can no longer hold the dissolved calcite. So it deposits solid calcite back into the cave, making splendid structures in the process.

Water continues to seep through cracks in the cave's ceiling. With each drip, a little calcite is left behind on the ceiling. The calcite collects, speck by speck, to form hanging structures called stalactites. They grow very slowly—only about .08 inch (2 millimeters) or so a year.

In the early stages, stalactites may look like tiny tubes, or "soda straws." When the hollow tubes become clogged, the stalactites grow thicker and longer. Now they look like stone icicles.

Beneath the stalactites, water splashes on the cave floor. Calcite builds up splash by splash, and stalagmites begin to form. They often grow more than 50 feet (15 meters) high.

Eventually, a stalactite and stalagmite may meet to form a "column."

After trillions of drips and splashes—and perhaps millions of years—a stalactite eventually joins the stalagmite below it. When they join, the two form a column, also called a pillar.

Cave

A limestone cave may have many different kinds of cave structures, or speleothems. Some of the more interesting ones shown here are draperies, pearls, flowstone, helictites, and gypsum flowers. Minerals in the water add colorful stripes to some of these formations.

Cave pearls, it should be noted, are not real pearls. Real pearls form in oysters.

Draperies

Flowstone

Decorations

helictites

Calcite cave pearls form in pools around a grain of sand. Because the sand granule is kept in constant motion by the flowing water, a ball-shaped "pearl" begins to form.

A gypsum flower

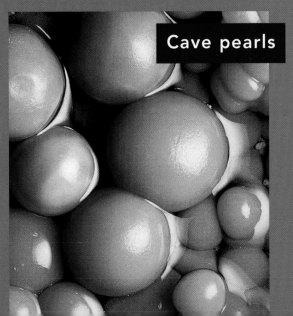

Cave pearls

Cave Animals

Caves are not the lifeless places you might imagine. Many different kinds of animals, both large and small, live in caves. Some animals, such as bats, spend only some of their time in caves. Others, like blindfish, spend their entire lives in there.

Bats flying
out of a cave

Many animals take shelter in
the entrance of a cave. Daylight
shines in this part of the cave,
and the cave protects the
animals from harsh weather.
Animals that take cover here

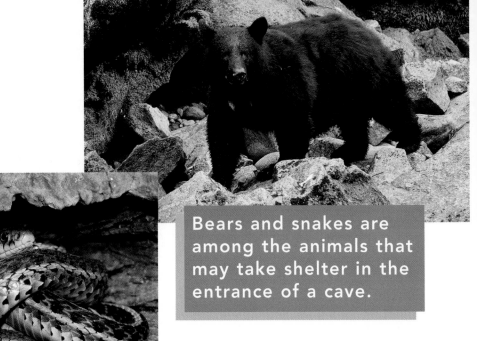

Bears and snakes are among the animals that may take shelter in the entrance of a cave.

include bears, raccoons, skunks, snakes, and mice.

Farther inside a cave is a place called the twilight zone. This part of the cave gets only dim light. This suits some kinds of owls, a variety of bats, and

Oilbirds (above) and some kinds of bats (left) live in a cave's twilight zone.

even a few birds, such as swiftlets and oilbirds. But these animals are visitors—they occupy the cave only temporarily.

Animals that spend their whole lives in caves live in the darkness beyond the twilight zone. They include certain kinds of insects, crayfish, salamanders, and fish. Generation after generation of these cave-dwellers, or troglodytes, have lived in total darkness. Because they live in the dark, they don't need to see. Many are blind, and some have no eyes at all. They use their strong senses of smell and touch instead.

These animals are colorless, too. Their bodies need no protection from sunlight in the darkness of a cave, so their skin needs no pigment.

Animals that live in the total darkness of a cave, such as (counterclockwise from above) this crayfish, spider, salamander, and millipede, are usually colorless.

Blind "Sight"

How do animals "see" in the murky darkness of a cave? Some animals, such as bats and swiftlets, avoid crashing by sending out sounds. When its sounds bounce off surrounding objects, the bat or swiftlet hears the echo and is guided by it. This kind of navigation is called echolocation.

Other animals, such as blind beetles, have very long, sensitive feelers, or antennae, to guide them in the darkness. The blindfish has ridges on the front and sides of its head that are sensitive to touch.

A blindfish

People and Caves

Thousands of years ago, people lived in the openings of caves. The caves provided shelter and protection.

Scientists exploring caves have discovered bits of pottery and evidence of ancient campfires. Some archaeologists—scientists who study

Visitors to a cave where
humans once lived

early life—believe that the
Anasazi may have built their
dwellings in caves to protect
themselves from invaders.

In 1940, four boys acci-
dentally discovered Lascaux
Cave in France. Its walls were

decorated with ancient paintings of bulls, horses, and deer. The cave was not a living space, and archaeologists cannot agree on why the paintings

Ancient paintings on the walls of Lascaux Cave in France

were made. Did early people believe the paintings had magical powers? We may never know the answer, but we do know that Lascaux and other decorated caves were special places.

Indeed, caves are special places. They are also easily damaged. When people explore caves, they change them forever. Sometimes people break stalactites just to carry home a souvenir. Lint

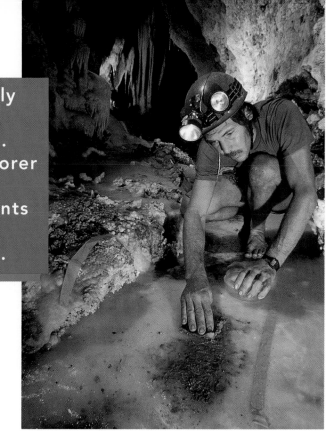

Caves are easily damaged by human visitors. This cave explorer is cleaning off muddy footprints left behind by earlier visitors.

and seeds may fall from people's clothing. And lightbulbs are sometimes used to light up show caves for tourists. These lights then enable green plants to grow. The

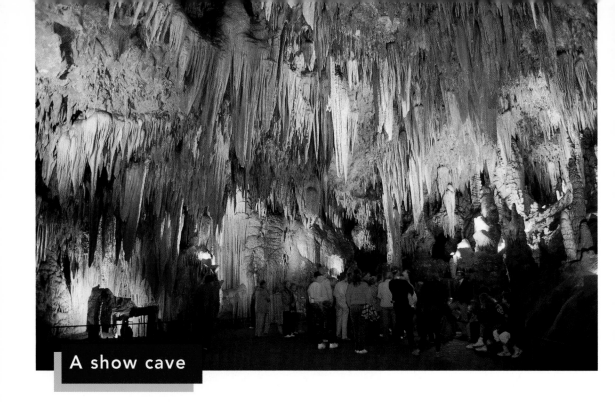

A show cave

added light also can damage
wall paintings. For this reason,
the original Lascaux Cave has
been closed to the public.

Caves are strange and
spectacular parts of our planet.
They have taken millions of

years to become what they are. Only our respect for them will guarantee that they have an unspoiled and natural future.

Caves are natural wonders that need to be protected and preserved.

To Find Out More

Here are some additional resources to help you learn more about caves:

 **Books**

Gallant, Roy A. **Limestone Caves.** Franklin Watts, 1998.

Gibbons, Gail. **Caves and Caverns.** Harcourt Brace & Company, 1993.

Schultz, Ron. **Looking Inside Caves and Caverns.** John Muir Publications, 1993.

Silver, Donald M. **Cave** (One Small Square series). W.H. Freeman and Co., 1993.

☀ Organizations and Online Sites

American Cave Museum
119 E. Main Street
Horse Cave, KY 42749
*http://www.cavern.org/
museum.htm*

Includes exhibits on modern cave exploration, prehistoric cave explorers, the history of Mammoth Cave, and much more.

Cave Ecology
*http://www.kdu.com/
caveecol.html*

Learn about how caves are formed and how caves and the land in which they are located are closely tied together. Includes a glossary of cave terms, caving tips, and student activities.

The Chauvet-Pont-d'Arc Cave
*http://mistral.culture.fr/
culture/arcnat/chauvet/
en/gvpda-d.htm*

Information about and photos of a painted cave that was discovered in France in 1994.

Virtual Cave
*http://www.goodearth.com
/virtcave.html*

View images of minerals unique to caves, see a list of caves that you can visit, and take a virtual tour of an actual cave.

Important Words

carbonic acid compound formed when rainwater picks up and dissolves carbon dioxide; it is the agent that dissolves limestone to form limestone caves

decaying rotting, breaking apart

deposit to drop

dwellings homes

groundwater water within the Earth that supplies wells and springs

mineral natural substance that is not a plant or animal

particles very small parts, pieces, or amounts

pigment coloring matter in humans, animals, and plants

water table top level of water stored in the ground

Index

Meet the Author

Larry Dane Brimner is a former teacher who now writes full time for children. He is the author of numerous titles for Children's Press. If you enjoyed this book, you'll probably also enjoy his Children's Press books *Geysers, Glaciers,* and *Mountains.* When he isn't writing or speaking to children and teachers, Larry can usually be found at his desk in San Diego, California.